Dangerous Worship

Book #5 in the Little Book Series

Kent Philpott
Katie Philpott

EVP

Dangerous Worship

©2020 by Kent Philpott

All rights reserved.
Earthen Vessel Media, LLC
San Rafael, CA 94903
earthenvesselmedia.com

ISBN: 978-1-946794-18-5 print
ISBN: 978-1-946794-19-2 EPUB
Library of Congress Control Number: 2020939137

Cover and interior design by KLC Philpott

All Biblical Scripture quotations, unless otherwise indicated, are taken from the Holy Bible, English Standard Version® (ESV®), copyright © 2001 by Crossway Bibles, a publishing ministry of Good News Publishers. All rights reserved.

Other books in the Little Book Series:
Biblical Christianity Is Evangelical
The Preposterous God
Spiritual Health
What's So Bad about Hell?

Contents

Introduction

Are there experts on the subject of worship?

Maybe there are; I am not one of these. With what little I bring to the table, I must rely on my understanding of the Bible along with my personal experience and research to speak to the massive subject of worship. Why? Because I am convinced there is both safe and dangerous worship.

The word worship is based on the term worth. To worship, then, is to pay homage to or revere some person or thing or event that has worth. The ultimate or highest worship is to pay homage to, revere, or worship God, whom we define as the Creator of all that is and who alone has power and is ultimate Judge over all His creation.

This is a Little Book consisting mostly of essays that I have written over the years relating to the subject. Some will be more exactly to the point than others.

The first essay here is "Dangerous Worship," which is not a frivolous subject. Would anyone want to spend their lives honoring or worshiping that which is false or imaginary?

Let us take the atheist, for instance. What if, contrary to their view, there is a God? Then that person's whole life is far less than it could have been. Conversely, what if there is no god, as the atheist is counting on? Will he or she not find a substitute to worship?

How about the theists who may avow some sort of higher power, but will not be definite about it? Who or what do they worship? Take your pick. As Bob Dylan wrote, "You are going to serve someone. It may be the devil, it may be the Lord, but you are going to serve someone."

For adherents of some religions, for example Hinduism, the gods and goddesses are myriad. At what is their reverence directed? Any and all of these gods? What if they forget some?

There is a Book, which is what the word Bible means, that boldly proclaims that there is a Creator God who has revealed Himself via the lives and testimonies of real people as recorded from Genesis to Revelation, thus making Himself known.

Over time, His creation moved toward the worship of idols and demons instead of the true and living God. The word "sin" is applied to these events. Despite that, He sent His only Son to die for these misdirected and ultimately deadly errors of the worshipers of false gods. This is called love, agape love, of which only the Triune God is capable.

His power, majesty, and love are why Christians worship the God of the Bible. This makes ultimate sense to us, and this worship is actually commanded by God, because He knows what we will do if we do not worship Him. Yes, we go astray, dangerously so, and worship whomever and whatever seems right in our own eyes.

So, worship is critically important, and this is why I put these essays together. My hope is that it will be of some value to you.

Dangerous Worship

Snooky Lanson, Russell Arms, Dorothy Collins, Gisele MacKenzie, and the rest of the Hit Parade gang were all on 1950s television programs, and I could not miss an episode. I still sing, "Three Coins in a Fountain" and "How Much is that Doggie in the Window." That was then.

Along came Bill Haley and the Comets with "Rock Around the Clock," and I was captured. "Rock and Roll is Here to Stay" (Danny & the Juniors), was a song I will never forget—a profound prophecy.

At El Monte Legion Stadium in El Monte, California, Chuck Berry crouch walked across the stage giving us "Johnny B. Goode," and we screamed and yelled. And then it got better and better. With heavy bass, electric guitar, and drums pounding, the pieces grew longer and longer, and we were mesmerized, movin' and groovin' to the beat. We could not get enough.

This is now. Show up at the local church and hear the same movin' and groovin' sort of music with Jesus thrown in occasionally, if you can make out the lyrics. At least the music is Christianized. (Not sure if this is good or bad.)

During the 1970s, I learned how to strum eight cords with my Conqueror guitar (Japanese imitation of the

Gibson Hummingbird) along with our little band, Joyful Noise. We stayed together for four years and toured through several states with our version of Gospel Rock, badly done. Our songs were "Jesus, Jesus, When I Hear that Golden Name," "You'll Never Get to Heaven on LSD," "I Kinda Like the Christian Way of Life" (stolen from a Byrds song), and a rock version of "This Little Light of Mine." I have a photo of our band playing at San Quentin State Prison in 1971, a photo I highly prize. We got a standing O.

I never quit. This coming Sunday during worship service our little "band" will be doing two songs accompanied by an electric bass, a mandolin, and a piano, with my wife Katie working a djembe drum. And I will be holding the Conqueror, which has a pick-up in it. We will play "I Woke Up This Morning with my Mind Stayed on Jesus" and "I'm So Glad Jesus Set Me Free." Following will be our small choir doing a traditional or Black Gospel piece. Total elapsed time, maybe fifteen minutes.

The Game Changer

John Wimber and the Church Growth series at Fuller Theological Seminary in Pasadena, California, in the late 1980s, changed everything for way too many of us. He had a program for those who already were used to groovin' in the Spirit and a much longer one for those who were new to "real worship." The lighting was also very important. The idea was to get folks into a mood, a mindset, where they could feel the power in the room. I say "power" not "Spirit" since I am not sure it was the Holy Spirit who "showed up." I think it rarely was. My more experienced thinking says it was the same scenario as at the El Monte Legion Stadium back in my youth—the same sensation of movin' and groovin' to the beat.

By this time in my life I have attended many wild and crazy worship services, several at the Bethel Church in Redding, California, and several more at a church in Marin County that is affiliated with Bethel. Everyone has a high time, "tokin' on the Spirit" or "drunk in the Spirit," which are phrases used by these worshipers, and when stoned in the Spirit, anything can happen. People report visions or angels speaking to them; they might download "a word" for someone present in the room, crash and burn on the floor, and dance, dance, dance. Well, isn't that what King David did?

Dare we ask whether this sort of thing is biblically oriented worship? My suspicion is that so much of what goes under the rubric of worship is little more than an endorphin-infused high.

The Worship Service

One never knows what one might find at a church worship service. Some may be structured in traditional format with written prayers like The Collect of the Day, the Lord's Prayer, an answer and response call to worship, a doxology sung, and a reciting of the Apostles' Creed. This fairly well describes what it looks like at Miller Avenue Baptist Church of Mill Valley, of which I am pastor, but we do include a couple of more contemporary songs as described above. But if this particular church were up to date and seeking young people, that is anyone under sixty, it would look like the following:

A focus would be on feelings, attempting to reach a high and good feeling level that is supposedly a sense of the inner working of the Holy Spirit. Without that high it would be assumed that the Holy Spirit never "showed up." Never mind that Jesus said that where two or three are gathered together in His name there He is in their midst (see Matthew 18:20). But old rock-and-rollers like what seems like a spiritual high—that sense of being a little, if not a lot, "out of it." Along have come the young rock-and-rollers who suppose this is what real Christian worship must be.

A kind of prayer time is inserted, too, but it has little resemblance to traditional and biblical prayer. What my experience has shown me multiple times is that prayer involves thinking, personal examination, and reflecting on core teachings of Jesus. These, along with shouts of praise phrases like "hallelujah, praise God, glory, glory, glory, and so on can combine but stay well under control and managed.

My first prayer meetings

I have been in hundreds of prayer meetings, some short, some very long. Here is what I experienced personally as a new believer.

At First Baptist Church in Fairfield, California, where I was converted, the prayer meeting was held on Wednesday nights. The pastor, Bob Lewis, spoke to those gathered together about some aspect of prayer for ten or fifteen minutes. Then there was group prayer for another twenty or so minutes, with various people voicing requests, petitions, and often confessions of personal sin. Following would be a time of individual prayer.

We understood that Jesus was with us right then and there. We got on our knees and prayed silently for about half an hour. Sometimes there were shedding of tears, and nobody did anything or said anything about it. It was personal and dignified. We closed out with a hymn and the Lord's Prayer.

I am not suggesting that this be the pattern, but it was real prayer. We made our requests known to God; our eyes, hearts, and minds were on Jesus, and we concluded with the prayer Jesus taught us to pray. And usually we left silently, reverently, and at peace. How I miss those times.

I wonder

A number of times I wondered what spirit was present when things simply got wild and crazy. Was it all just the beat of the drum, the lighting, the urging by the worship leader, and people falling out? Was it nothing more than party time as I had seen in the Kirtans of the Hare Krishna devotees at the temple on Fredrick Street in San Francisco's Haight-Ashbury District that I attended in the winter and spring of 1967?[1] I have been in many a "prayer and worship service" that was not dissimilar from what the hippie Hare Krishna devotees were doing.

I wondered then what spirit or spirits might be lurking in that Hindu temple back then, and I wonder the same thing about some of the prayer and worship meetings I have witnessed firsthand at some of the churches in the movement.[2]

I have often heard the case made that churches that do not move in the Spirit, with no "fire" pouring down—

---

[1] Swami Bhaktivedanta would allow me to conduct a Bible study in the basement of the temple only as long as I attend the Kirtan first. And so I did. A Kirtan consisted of three half-hour chants like Hare Krishna, Hare Krishna, Hare, Hare, Krishna, Krishna and on and on while dancing to the Hindu style live music.

[2] See my book, *False Prophets Among Us: What is the New Apostolic Reformation and Why is it Dangerous?* It is available at Amazon.com.

meaning those who have calm and orderly worship and prayers services—are both boring and spiritually dead. I have heard this time and again, and this way of thinking is characteristic of the cultic mindset. This is spiritual superiority, a we-versus-they mentality, and I understand this, because for a decade I thought in the very same way.

Lessons from history

During the middle of the second century there arose a movement that history has named Montanism, which would, in our era, be considered charismatic/Pentecostal in doctrine and practice. It was a dangerous departure from the church that emerged during the days of the New Testament's Book of Acts.

Consider another group, this one from the first quarter of the sixteenth century, led by Thomas Munster. Munster was a noted leader of the early Anabaptist movement and produced a serious distortion of Anabaptists known as the radical reformation. They tried to reform Christianity beyond the limits of Luther, Zwingli, and Calvin's work. Their practices mirror some of that which is currently found in highly "spiritual" worship, for example, in churches associated with the New Apostolic Reformation such as Bethel Church in Redding, California.

Neither of these groups, the Montanists or the Munsterites, survived long, which is mostly due to their spiritual excesses. My point is that it is dangerous to go beyond the practices we find in the New Testament. The Church at Corinth, early on, developed forms of church life that caused the Apostle Paul to write to them in hopes of mitigating some dangerous forms of worship there.

There are other examples as well; my point is that from time to time dangerous forms of worship develop, and we are now witnessing it yet again, but on a scale unprecedented in comparison to anything else I know of in our Christian history.

There is such a strong pull for that which makes us feel good, and this sensation is assumed to be part of what worship is all about. I embraced such a notion myself, so I am not one to cast stones. However, it is necessary to call attention to aberrations in our faith and worship.

Christianity is not the only faith system with ecstatic forms of worship. Shia Islam has the whirling dervishes. Judaism has its mystical Kabbalah worship. Buddhism has the drumming and mind-emptying meditation. The shamans around the world have their hallucinatory drugs along with drumming. The Santeríans have their bembe, using both drumming and dancing to induce the trance state, and the list goes on. The issue for biblically oriented Christians is, can such worship be supported from Scripture?

Worship in the Bible

David danced, as we find in 2 Samuel 6:14-15. This was in celebration of the return of the Ark of the Covenant.

And David danced before the LORD with all his might. And David was wearing a linen ephod. So David and all the house of Israel brought up the ark of the LORD with shouting and with the sound of the horn.

Then in Psalm 149:1-3 and Psalm 150, authors unknown, we find evidence of dancing with musical instruments played while praising God.

Psalm 149:1–3

Praise the LORD!
Sing to the LORD a new song,
his praise in the assembly of the godly!
Let Israel be glad in his Maker;
let the children of Zion rejoice in their King!
Let them praise his name with dancing,
making melody to him with tambourine and lyre!

Psalm 150

Praise the LORD!
Praise God in his sanctuary;
praise him in his mighty heavens!
Praise him for his mighty deeds;
praise him according to his excellent greatness!
Praise him with trumpet sound;
praise him with lute and harp!

> Praise him with tambourine and dance;
> praise him with strings and pipe!
> Praise him with sounding cymbals;
> praise him with loud clashing cymbals!
> Let everything that has breath praise the LORD!
> Praise the LORD!

Moving to the New Testament, we find no reference to dancing, yet we do see singing and music.

Ephesians 6:18–20

> And do not get drunk with wine, for that is debauchery, but be filled with the Spirit, addressing one another in psalms and hymns and spiritual songs, singing and making melody to the Lord with your heart, giving thanks always and for everything to God the Father in the name of our Lord Jesus Christ, submitting to one another out of reverence for Christ.

Colossians 3:16–17

> Let the word of Christ dwell in you richly, teaching and admonishing one another in all wisdom, singing psalms and hymns and spiritual songs, with thankfulness in your hearts to God. And whatever you do, in word or deed, do everything in the name of the Lord Jesus, giving thanks to God the Father through him.

What these "psalms and hymns and spiritual songs"

consisted of is unknown. Likely no drums, electric strings, or bass guitar, but instruments common to the day were played. And we find no mention of dancing. No movin' and groovin' to the beat. No wild, ecstatic, trance-inducing efforts being made, and no worship leader urging people to press in, go deeper, and get more of God.

There is little information about how the early church worshiped. It certainly would have had no similarity to the kind of alcohol/drug inspired worship found in pagan temples of that day.

There are no encouragements by the Bible writers to go deeper and tune in, plug into the Spirit, and listen for the voice of God. What is seen in much of the worship in the churches associated with the New Apostolic Movement and other churches promoting a drone-style type of worship cannot be affirmed in Scripture. Just the opposite!

The Development of Dangerous Worship

To worship means to bow down before God and acknowledge Him as Lord. This worship may take place anywhere and does not require a band, a worship leader, proper lighting, or swinging and swaying to the beat of the drum. Worship may be corporate, or it may be individual. Being alone, in private, on one's knees, if not in form then in attitude, a follower of Jesus may bow before his or her Maker. When we think we have to be in a certain frame of mind, feeling spiritual, with eyes closed, while shouting praises and waving our arms in the air, we are not attuned to biblical worship. No, this is contemporary, culture-imposed, counterfeit worship. And where this occurs, spirits may indeed show up and manifest their demonic presence in various ways. Yes, that is correct: "demonic presence."

What I have observed in numbers of "worship services" is comparable to the dances of the whirling dervishes, Hindu ecstatic worshipers, shamanistic based celebrations, Santerían bembes, even satanic rituals. Here worshipers get high in the spirit, not generated by drugs, but by processes whereby the mind is moved into another world. Nothing is done decently and in order. There is a cacophony of so-called "words of prophecy" being shouted loudly but which no one hears; add to that the downloads being broadcast widely and wildly, people falling out and crashing on the floor and sometimes for hours, and plenty of jumping up and down. Again, I must say: This is not of the Holy Spirit of God.

Once indoctrinated into this false spirituality, it carries over into the rest of one's life. Hearing voices, getting words for others, finding out supernaturally how one should respond to this or that goes on, often to the point where one's mental capacity is impacted. And here the terms passive state of mind, shamanistic state of mind, and altered state of consciousness come into play.

States of Consciousness

Substance abusers, and even those who simply enjoy "downing a few," understand and value the temporary relief given by mind numbing concoctions. Something similar can be achieved in dangerous worship. There are no Twelve Step programs for these, though I can imagine that in the near future there may be a need for such.[3]

Imagine letting go and floating and dancing along with the band, all the while apparently reaching new highs of spirituality. Nearly or maybe fully out of control but convinced it is all for the praise and worship of God. Anything goes, since it is all covered by the "anointing," and who would oppose the "anointing?" Opposing the "anointing" could offend the Holy Spirit, and one might be close to blasphemy, right?

Is there no guardian on the premises? The cry goes out, "Touch not mine anointed!" That stops critical thinking and gives license to many bizarre behaviors. Voicing a critique is akin then to blasphemy of the Holy Spirit, with the conclusion that such would be akin to

---

[3] At this point, March of 2020 there is news of recovery groups being formed for those who are falling out of this sort of dangerous worship churches and groups.

suppressing the move of God. License given.

There is reward, too. Wow, the Spirit is using so and so who just recently was reticent and retiring but is now under the power. Never mind the strange words given to others; one must not question these, prophecies such as, "God woke me up at 3 a.m. and told me to tell you that you will have a worldwide healing ministry." Oh, the celebration!

I wish I had a count of those who have been given "words," "messages," "revelations," and "divine guidance," along the lines that they were being honored with a great and wonderful ministry. I wonder about how it is for the recipients of such anointed words when things don't turn out as prophesied?

Dangerous worship, as found in so many demonically oriented religious movements, can bring a person into an altered state of consciousness, one where the normal boundaries to invasion by evil spirits are broken down. Once the normal protective barriers are down, demonic possession can begin.

A characteristic of many who are demon oppressed/possessed is hyper spirituality. No one is as spiritual. In my pastoral ministry, I have seen "anointed ones" develop relationships with those who are suffering with mental instability and take these unhappy brothers or sisters under their hideous guidance, all in the name of Jesus.

My dear friends, beware of the altered states of conscience: what looks to be genuinely spiritual is not necessarily so.

The Cultic Mentality

It was 1976. I was riding high, among those blessed with power and knowledge. Then I hit a wall with full impact. The major professor in my doctrinal program, an acknowledged expert in cults and the cultic mentality, pulled me aside one day and politely and gently told me that the church I pastored was cultic. The next week I brought him our church's statement of faith. A week later, having carefully read through this document, he told me our theology was mainstream enough. The problem was our view of who we were.

I have to acknowledge that this was not the first time I had heard such. Two professors during my years at Golden Gate Baptist Seminary in Mill Valley, CA, where I was enrolled in a ThM program, warned me about virtually the same danger. But I disregarded their counsel. Then, in 1978, I knew it was all true. I had become captive to a cultic mentality.

Here is how it looked: I was moving in the Spirit. I spoke in tongues. People were healed when I laid my hands on them. Casting out of demos was routine. There were words of knowledge and prophecies galore. Youth were flocking in, and we were the largest evangelical/Pentecostal/charismatic church in Marin County. Don't tell me!

The issue was my view of our church versus other churches. The truth is, I looked down on them and did not speak brotherly or biblically of them to others. We were where the Spirit was moving. And of course, it was only a matter of time before it all came crashing down. There is more to the story, but this is enough for now.

From 1988 to 1994, I led a cult recovery support group. Each session lasted six months, which equaled twelve times through the process. How very painful it was. At the end of it, I was not fully recovered, and likely that is true to this day, but I am making progress, however slowly. Here is where I learned the signs of the cultic mentality.

Once we think and claim to have a special anointing, one which others do not have, we become highly defensive with those who disagree with us and hope to call us to account. They become enemies, darts of the devil, and the working of the antichrist in these last days. And much of all this begins with dangerous worship.

Safe, Biblical Worship

Biblical worship is directed to the only God: the Father, Son, and Holy Spirit. We mindfully give praise and thanksgiving for His grace and mercy. Worship comes from our core, our hearts and minds, regardless of, often despite, our feelings. Worship does not and should not have to be "worked up" through the use of music, dance, or anything else.

Worship to God may be made in a gathering or when alone. Praise and adoration may be voiced or thought, whether feeling "blessed" or not. For centuries the early church, often during severe persecutions, worshiped the God and Father of our Lord Jesus Christ in the worst of conditions, even while being burned at the stake or torn apart by wild beasts.

If one has to be led into worship; if one has to be motivated by external factors before there is worship, is this actual worship? I am not afraid to answer, No! It is something, but it is not biblical worship, and thus it is not safe.

At the Kirtan, the Hare Krishna worship services that I attended in 1967 at the temple on Fredrick Street in San Francisco's Haight-Ashbury District, I was certain there were spirits present, but I knew none was the Holy Spirit. How can I make such a claim? Over the years, a ministry we call "deliverance" developed. This casting out of demons was part and parcel of our regular ministry, and it continues today, though not nearly as often as then, thankfully.[4] Those who had engaged

---

[4] Two years ago, our Earthen Vessel Media published

24

in those Kirtans danced to the inspiration of demonic spirits. I know this, because we cast out demons from some of those devotees. Their worship was dangerous.

Do I suspect that the wild and crazy worship fueled by the beat of the drum, the twang of the guitar, and the urging of a worship leader could possibly be dangerous? Yes, I do!

The reality is that we are on dangerous ground when we move beyond the clear boundaries of biblical worship. Whenever there needs be external stimulus in order for worship to happen, then there is danger.

Worship at Miller Avenue Baptist Church in Mill Valley is quite boring. We are liturgical, and by that I mean we say a Call to Worship according to the church calendar, sing the Deuteronomic Shema, recite the Apostles' Creed, recite the Collect of the Day, sing the Gloria Patri and the standard doxology, and end with the Aaronic Benediction. We sing several standard hymns, and the little band plays a couple of old choruses. All the way along there is worship, and the sermon is usually a verse by verse exposition of a passage of Scripture. It is certainly safe!

Am I Judging other Christians?

Over the years I have been accused of judging my

brothers and sisters in Christ when I question various forms of worship in which they participate.

Warning, yes, encouraging evaluation, yes, but judging, no. To judge is to pass sentence upon those who are guilty. We have our lawyers and judges, but these do not operate in the courts of heaven. Only God can and will judge.

The Scripture is full of "thou shalt nots" and warnings, and more. Simply read through the Sermon on the Mount in Matthew chapters 5, 6, and 7. When we preach the Good News to the lost, we bring up the ultimate danger of unforgiven sin. We must do this; it is our work, for without it the evangelical message is incomplete. Is it loving to avoid the bad news that there is a god of this world who blinds the minds of those who are not safe in Christ? (see 2 Corinthians 4:4). Is it loving to ignore danger signals?

I have admitted that I had been captured by a cultic mindset. Even when I was warned about some of my dangerous views I reacted and spoke badly of those who challenged my super spirituality while being sure these critics were not likewise "spirit filled." These seminary professors warned me because they loved me and cared enough to reach out to me. I am hoping, dear reader, that this is what and why I am presenting this Little Book.

The Anointing. The Anointing. The Anointing.

"The Anointing — this is the whole thing, isn't it?"

That is what I heard Paul Cain say some ten years ago at a nearby Pentecostal church.

Reverend Cain is a big name among the so-called Kansas City Prophets, along with a number of others like Bob Jones, Mike Bickel, Rick Joiner, John Paul Jackson, Francis Frangipane, Lou Engle, and James Goll. The Apostolic-Prophetic Movement[1], sometimes known as the Third Wave, was to be the re-establishment of the Five-Fold ministry of apostle, prophet, evangelist, pastor and teacher as found in Ephesians 4[2]. These

---

[1] C. Peter Wagner is often recognized as an "apostle" in the recreation of the "Five Fold Ministry," and by virtue of his position as a professor at Fuller Theological Seminary in Pasadena, California, and his part in launching the Church Growth seminars at Fuller (of which I was a part), he provided prestige and clout to the fledgling "Third Wave" revival.

[2] Rather than 5 ministries of apostle, prophet, evangelist, pastor, and teacher, many combine pastor and teacher, since the two are joined by the Greek co-coordinating conjunction kai meaning "and". More correctly, it is the four fold ministry. And it may be noted that, while these ministries or offices may not always have been formally established,

leaders see themselves as part of the reconstitution of the fabled biblical model meant to operate in the "last days." And for such a grand vision, a special and super powerful anointing would be required.

Rodney M. Howard-Browne

I was wondering then if the anointing Cain talked about was the same that Rodney M. Howard-Browne purportedly brought to America from his home in South Africa. It was Howard-Browne who strongly influenced the "revival" that came to the Toronto Airport Vineyard Church in Canada in the 1990s. It was there that Randy Clark received the anointing from Howard-Browne and spread the "fire" of the revival.

Howard-Browne, in his books Flowing in the Holy Ghost (FHG) and Flowing in the Holy Spirit (FHS), describes that anointing.[3] It is essential and necessary to define what Howard-Browne means by anointing as presented in the two books mentioned above.

In FHG he says, "the anointing is the presence of God" …"that will come and begin to touch people" (p. 13). "I wait for the unction all the time; I wait for the burning of the Spirit of God within. That burning, that churning,

---

they have never be absent in the long history of the Church.

[3] The two books are virtually identical in content, having only minor variations and additions. To read one is to read the other.

28

bubbles like a boiling pot inside, because that's what the word 'prophesy' means" (p. 14).

Howard-Browne says, "you must stir yourself up for the gifts to begin to operate" (p. 14). Therefore, after stirring, "it will happen automatically. God will begin to move." (p. 15).

In a section labeled "When the Anointing Falls" he says, "I began to speak supernaturally. I became another person! . . .It's almost like I'm standing outside my body, hearing myself prophesy. . . . People begin to shake and fall out under the power of God in their seats as the word of the Lord comes forth. No one touches them" (p. 31). He goes on: "You can't say, 'I'm going to get up and prophesy now.' However, you can prepare for the anointing to prophesy. You do this by stirring yourself up, by preparing your heart, and by waiting on the Spirit of God. Then, when the anointing comes, you flow with it. But you can only prophesy when the anointing comes!'" (p. 31).

Randy Clark

Not everyone got the anointing, not even those who actually touched Howard-Browne. Randy Clark, who had reportedly gotten the anointing, was also able to pass it on to others, or so it was claimed. Clark was in Toronto, too, and people touched him; and some got it, but most didn't.

A contingent from our local ministerial association visited Toronto, and after they returned we gathered in a meeting. There we were, expecting something big. But even for those who got close to the "anointed" people and even touched one of them, nothing happened. Though disappointed, we planned another trip.

I saw Randy Clark personally some years back now in Redding, California, when he visited the Bethel Church pastored by Bill Johnson, whom I guessed had gotten the anointing as well. The anointing was power, and power was what it was all about, the power to heal and do miracles. Many members of Bethel had miracle stories to tell: crowns of gold on teeth; gold dust in their hair; feathers mysteriously floating down from the ceiling; people raised from the dead (none were confirmed); people with stomach and back pain – healed; folks with chronic migraines – healed; youth who smoked pot and were popping pills – healed on the spot. Oddly, the people I was with who were members of Bethel, both with some serious bodily ailments, were never themselves healed, nor did they know anyone personally who had actually been healed. The miracle stories circulated around town, one here, one there, but somehow the ones healed could not be located. This was no doubt a miracle, too.

Do I sound irreverent or judgmental? Am I being a God mocker and thus in danger of committing blasphemy against the Holy Spirit?[4] Could I be standing against the flowing of the river of the Spirit now moving in these last days? Am I foolishly, even rebelliously, refusing to ride the wave? Frankly, these kinds of mind-think, conformist charges are enough to satisfy and shut-up most questioners, but not everyone is falling in line or is so lacking in confidence in the saving grace of Jesus that they stop thinking and evaluating.

Cain's anointing

Paul Cain rambled on for an hour and finally stated he was about to reveal the biggee, the real deal, the ultimate, that one great thing that meant absolutely everything. Wow, the anticipation; it was palpable. Cain moved toward the front of the stage. He stood stone still. He stretched out his left arm, his brown eyes scanning the congregation, while we waited without a sound. And then it came, what we were all waiting for: "The Anointing. The Anointing. The Anointing." He said it was the anointing.

To demonstrate the anointing he stared at a number of the faithful sitting in the front row.[5] One by one he

---

[4] The God Mockers is the title of a book written by Stephen Hill who was the principle evangelist for the Brownsville Revival in Pensacola, Florida during the mid-1990s. All those who rejected the idea that it was a genuine outpouring of the Holy Spirit he so labeled.

[5] I had gotten in place early and was a little surprised to

31

described what would happen to them in the future, essentially telling their fortunes. He said he saw a television set type thing over each one's head and could watch their futures unfold before his very eyes. One would be a great prophet in Africa. Another would be greatly used of God in Asia as a healer. One young lady would found a school for orphans in South America. Without exception each person would do something great and wonderful in the kingdom of God. Cain could see it on the television screen. It was the anointing that made it all happen.

Kundalini and Shaktipat

Over the years I've talked with a number of so-called prophets and healers who spoke like Howard-Browne. A burning power rising up in their bodies that gave them power to do miracles was how it worked. During my days in the Jesus People Movement when we did see miracles, I never experienced or heard anything like what Howard-Browne described. However, I had, and actually continue to have, conversations with those involved in various spiritual practices that do sound like Howard-Browne's anointing. I turned to Wikipedia for the material I suspected I would find.

---

see ushers bring in a group of people and seat them in the front row directly in front of the platform. The reason for this became clear later on.

Kundalini is described within—*Eastern religious, or spiritual, tradition* as "an indwelling spiritual energy that can be awakened in order to purify the subtle system and ultimately to bestow the state of Yoga, or Divine Union, upon the 'seeker' of truth." "The Yoga Upanishads describe Kundalini as lying 'coiled' at the base of the spine, represented as either a goddess or sleeping serpent waiting to be awakened." In physical terms, one commonly reported Kundalini experience is a feeling like electric current running along the spine.

Kundalini can be awakened by shaktipat -- spiritual transmission by a Guru or teacher -- or by spiritual practices such as yoga or meditation. Sometimes Kundalini reportedly awakens spontaneously as the result of physical or psychological trauma, or even for no apparent reason.

One man said he felt an activity at the base of his spine starting to flow so he relaxed and allowed it to happen. A feeling of surging energy began traveling up his back, at each chakra he felt an orgasmic electric feeling like every nerve trunk on his spine beginning to fire. A second man describes a similar experience but accompanied by a wave of euphoria and happiness softly permeating his being. He described the surging energy as being like electricity traveling from the base of his spine to the top of his head. He said the more he analyzed the experience, the less it occurred.

Kundalini can also awaken spontaneously, for no obvious reason; or it can be triggered by intense personal experiences such as accidents, near death experiences, childbirth, emotional trauma, extreme mental stress, and so on. Some sources attribute spontaneous awakenings to the "grace of God," or possibly to spiritual practice that occurred in past lives.

The popularization of eastern spiritual practices has been associated with psychological problems in the West. Psychiatric literature notes that "since the influx of eastern spiritual practices and the rising popularity of meditation starting in the 1960s, many people have experienced a variety of psychological difficulties, either while engaged in intensive spiritual practice or 'spontaneously'.

I could go on, but I think the above is enough; however, one last observation might be of value. On the fourth page of the Wikipedia article on Kundalini is a section with the heading, "Physical and psychological effects." In brief, I list some of the items which are referred to as "Kundalini syndrome":

Involuntary jerks, tremors, shaking, itching, tingling, and crawling sensations; energy rushes or feelings of electricity circulating the body; intense heat (heating) or cold; trance-like and altered states of consciousness; disrupted sleep pattern; loss of appetite or overeating; mood swings with periods of depression or mania.

The quest for power

Certainly Howard-Browne and any of the Kansas City Prophets and those associated with Rick Joyner of Morningstar in North Carolina, Mike Bickle of IHOP in Kansas City, Bill Johnson at Bethel Church in Redding, California, or anyone else associated with the Third Wave would not knowingly embrace anything to do with Kundalini or shaktipat, but there is an obvious association if not direct connection. That association could well be the quest for power.

Power, the one great and overriding drive behind the occult, is the great lure. So much of the tragedy of humanity has been the direct result of a striving to acquire and retain power. The quest for magical powers to heal drives shamanism and religions like Santería. Neo-pagan religions like Wicca also focus on power to heal and perform magic. How thin the line can is that separates the occult and pagan from the biblically orthodox.

Anyone who has either read of or experienced first-hand a great moving of the Holy Spirit desires to see it happen again. Most of the time we have the normal Christian experience, which is most of the time. Awakenings and revival come and go according to the will of God. But this is not enough for many who need more, more, and more.

For certain people then it is thought we can precipitate

a revival or awakening. It is not that difficult to "work up" a crowd of charismatic/Pentecostals especially, but just about any grouping of people, with pulsating music, expectations of miracles, high excitement from a dynamic preacher, and pass it off as a genuine move of the Holy Spirit. We must not ever forget that the chief way of identifying authentic Christianity is that Jesus Christ and Him crucified is front and center.

Off the charts

But then I think: no, wait a minute. These guys up in Redding at Bethel and in Kansas City say we are "off the charts." Their prophets declare that these are the last days and the Bible is not so important anymore. After all, many are conversing with angels now, even big name angels, some speaking directly with Jesus as one would in a phone call;[6] people like Kat Kerr are going direct to God, bypassing angels all together. Yes, face to face meetings with the Creator of heaven and earth in the "throne room" to get the real scoop for the last of the last days. Apparently, we are right up there at a few seconds before midnight on the great cosmic clock. Wow, I'm a believer!

---

[6] This is what Sarah Young does as she journals in her books like Jesus Calling.

Going corporate?

Am I making fun? Yes I am to a degree, in order to high-light the ridiculousness of the whole thing. And one wonders, what comes next? I mean, how can miracles be topped? After hearing from God personally and get-ting the definitive word about the wrap-up of history from the Big Guy, everything else seems second rate, not to mention a waste of time. A Christian friend liv-ing near the Bethel Church in Redding and who has followed the whole enterprise up to the present day said to me last month that there has been a shift into a "corporate" mode to fill a possible void, and by that he meant the selling of product – everything from wor-ship music, dietary supplements, t-shirts and other kinds of clothing, paperback books, and who knows what else that these entrepreneurs will concoct. God help us.

Is it possible for the newly and self-ordained apostles and prophets to change course? Think of the humilia-tion, the embarrassment, the decrease in salary, invi-tations to speak drying up, the rejections, the falling book sales, the payments due on the improvements to the property, the silence of the crowds? What do you do—retire, repent, step down, and confess, with your whole life exposed as a fraud? What do you do after making shipwreck of your faith and that of many thou-sands of others' faith as well? Here is where the mira-cles are needed.

Closing comment

I am one who has made major errors in my life and ministry, and from these I am yet greatly pained and will be until I get home. Indeed, the sufferings of this present time, whether the result of the Fall or my own rebellious folly, are not worth comparing with what God has prepared for us. My repenting will last my whole life, and though I may be embarrassed in certain circles, yet I take confidence that all my sin has been atoned for through the shedding of the precious blood of the Lamb. Thus it is with confidence that I continue following Jesus and rejoicing in the ability to yet be a servant in His kingdom. The audience, after all, is not in the pews but in heaven.

July, 2014

Healing, healing, healing—is it all about healing?

A significant part of Jesus' ministry involved healing. The motive for Jesus' healing ministry was compassion. "When he went ashore he saw a great crowd, and he had compassion on them and healed their sick" (Matthew 14:14). In John's Gospel, healing, along with other miracles, were also signs confirming that Jesus was the long-awaited Messiah.

It would seem that an emphasis on healing has taken center stage in many American churches. Some even think that if a church does not have a healing ministry, even specific healing rooms, it is deficient and that there must be something wrong with that church. This does not apply to all Christian churches in the USA, since the healing focus is still largely among Pentecostal and charismatic churches, but healing ministries, along with prosperity teaching, seem to be spilling over into churches that are neither Pentecostal nor charismatically inclined.

Why is this so? The most obvious reason may be that healing draws large numbers of people. It certainly did so in the ministry of Jesus. Many passages from the

Gospels could be quoted to verify this. However, simply because an emphasis on healing may attract crowds, that alone is not sufficient to justify a healing ministry. No, adhering to biblical precedent and faithfulness is foremost. Our work as Christians cannot be driven by seeming success in terms of 'nickels and noses.'

Whatever we do must clearly conform to established biblical methodology. My point is that the current popularity of healing ministries is not grounded in Scripture.

Miracles, miracles, miracles

People will traverse the globe hoping to see a miracle. This has long been known, and it is not to be associated only with the past. Places like Lourdes in France have been internationally famous for centuries and provide millions of pilgrims with the hope of a cure. Today thousands flock to churches and ministries that focus on healing, often with nothing other than a desire to witness a miracle. Certainly, many either have a need for some sort of healing or have loved ones who do. This is understandable.

Why do people like me then caution against seeking the miracle of healing? Notice the word "caution" as it is not wrong to seek God for healing.

One reason is that abuses may easily occur under such circumstances. People are so eager to be healed that such will be claimed when, in fact, no healing took place. This can be dangerous. Based on what I have found, miracles are claimed without any verification that an actual healing corrected an actual injury.

Another reason is that healing ministries are vulnerable to what I call "mind bending." Healings will be reported when none occurred, simply to support a healer and avoid the emotional conflict associated with cognitive dissonance. Few are able to protest in front of a congregation that is rooting for both the healer and the subject of the healing. Most will simply go along. Standing in the midst of hundreds of people, I would likely "bend" to the obvious will and need of those watching.

And then, not all healings are from the Spirit of God. Jesus warned, "False christs and false prophets will arise and perform great signs and wonders, so as to lead astray, if possible, even the elect (Matthew 24:24). "Signs and wonders" is a phrase often used in the New Testament and included physical healing (see John 4:48; Acts 4:30; Acts 8:4-13). This warning came toward the end of Jesus' earthly ministry, and something akin to it came at the beginning. Consider what Jesus said in Matthew 7:21-23:

> "Not everyone who says to me, 'Lord, Lord,' will enter the kingdom of heaven, but the one who does the will of my Father who is in heaven. On that day many will say to me, 'Lord,

Lord, did we not prophesy in your name, and cast out demons in your name, and do many mighty words in your name?' And then will I declare to them, 'I never knew you; depart from me, you workers of lawlessness.'"

Paul spoke similarly in 2 Thessalonians 9. "The coming of the lawless one is by the activity of Satan with all power and false signs and wonders." This depiction of the end of history and the working of Satan would likely involve healing, since we see the phrase "signs and wonders" used here in the very same manner we see it used to describe actual healing by God's Spirit. Satan indeed is a counterfeiter.

A last reason to be cautious about the present, renewed, emphasis on healing is that it is a distraction from the central ministry of the Church. Jesus commanded His followers to preach the Gospel in what we call the "Great Commission." He did not command us to go about healing (see Matthew 28:18-20 and Acts 1:8), although the longer ending of Mark 16:9-20 does contain these words: "they will lay hands on the sick, and they will recover" (Mark 16:18). The longer endings of Mark are clearly later additions to the Gospel and not original, but most editions of the King James Version of the Bible do not reflect the lack of early manuscript evidence, so many who rely on that version believe the ending is authentic.

Those who challenge churches that focus on miracles

and healing will do so on the basis that there is little or no Gospel proclamation involved. And those intent upon a healing emphasis have dismissed the criticism by insisting that the Gospel is indeed preached along with the healing work. However, after reading the literature, attending meetings, and surveying the many blogs covering the healing efforts, I would deny that the presentation of the Gospel is anything more than a casual mention, and even then it is, in my opinion, not the purpose of the minister to preach salvation.

The primacy of preaching Jesus, His person and His work, is what marks an authentic Christian ministry. One may be healed and yet be unconverted. Witnessing a miracle, or being healed, is not the same as being born again. Even if someone is healed many times, he or she will one day die. Then there is the judgment, and heaven or hell will be the final outcome. Healing is of significance, but, as Paul understood, it is at best secondary: "For I decided to know nothing among you except Jesus Christ and him crucified" (1 Corinthians 2:2).

The hunger for miracles

Miracles are addictive—seeing one is not enough. The miracle work of Jesus produced some untoward attention as well. In John 2:23-25 are these very revealing words:

> Now when he was in Jerusalem at the Passover Feast, many believed in his name when they saw the signs that he was doing. But Jesus on his part did not entrust himself to them, because he knew all people and needed no one to bear witness about man, for he himself knew what was in man.

Though many "believed," it is apparent that the believing was not of a saving nature. Saving faith is trust in Jesus alone for salvation and not a cognitive acknowledgment that Jesus is a miracle worker. Thus Jesus, knowing the great desire humans had to witness the supernatural, refused to be caught up in the inordinate excitement.

Ah, to be a miracle worker

During the Jesus People Movement of the late 1960s and early 1970s, many of us did witness miracles, and healing was included in that mix of signs and wonders. For a period of several years I prayed for people to be healed, accompanied by anointing with oil and laying on of hands. The problem for me with the healing ministry was the notoriety it brought. It was overly intoxicating, but it was also short-lived. We watched the healings and other miracles wane, even cease, as the Jesus People Movement ebbed away. The experience of seeing these miracles disappear caused many of us to question ongoing charismatic claims, but I now think that one could even be a cessationist—believing that the charismatic gifts did not survive the apostolic period—and yet believe in healing. (I identified at that time as a charismatic, but I no longer would be considered such in the sense that the word is used today.)

Let it be noted that I am one who is very aware of the power of the devil to imitate miracles and produce counterfeit healings. In addition, I am aware of the power of suggestion, the placebo effect, and the fact that nearly 50% of all doctor's visits have to do with psychosomatic complaints rather than true disease. Even still, I will attest to being a witness to real miracles, including healing.

My concern here is that we do not throw the proverbial baby out with the bath water, that we keep what is biblically faithful and reject what which is not. My view of it is that the instruction of James 5:13-15 is normative for the Church in all ages:

> Is anyone among you suffering: Let him pray. Is anyone cheerful: Let him sing praise. Is anyone among you sick? Let him call for the elders of the church, and let them pray over him, anointing him with oil in the name of the Lord. And the prayer of faith will save the one who is sick and the Lord will raise him up. And if he has committed sins, he will be forgiven.

Some have argued that the letter of James is sub-Christian, a "right strawy epistle" as Martin Luther thought. However, even after considering the historical context lying behind the letter of James, my view of it is that it is not error that we have the small letter included in our canon of inspired Scripture.

Could it be that many biblically oriented Christians have ignored anything to do with healing, de-emphasized it at least, because it has been hijacked and abused by the wealth and health preachers?

Must we be charismatic faith healers?

When requested, I will yet pray for people to be healed, basing my action on James 5 and the general compassion-based ministry of Jesus. Very few, if any, are healed in these current times. In fact, I rarely even speak of healing. But it is often in the back of my mind that dear people in the congregation are ill and need attention.

Is there a format for healing ministry? Must one anoint with oil and lay hands on the person to be healed? Whose faith is operative, the person who needs healing or the one(s) doing the praying for healing? These questions are difficult to answer. Jesus used no set pattern in healing. Sometimes He healed from a distance, sometimes He simply commanded it, and sometimes He touched, spit, made clay, and so on. If we think certain procedures must be carried out, like oil anointing or hands laid on, we are coming dangerously close to magical thinking. This occult-oriented notion must be strictly avoided. Regarding whose faith is operative or how much is needed, we simply have the words, "the prayer of faith will save the one who is sick" (James 5:15). There is a mystery here, but the one who is prayed to is the One who heals. That much is certain.

Whether or not people are obviously, verifiably healed must not motivate my decision to pray for them to be healed. In the same manner, I will proclaim the grace and mercy of God in salvation, whether people are converted in front of me or not.

A plea

A simple plea: It is important for me not to break fellowship with my Reformed brethren who may not view things as I do. I am hoping that my willingness to engage in praying for people to be healed will be seen as an intramural debate among brethren, rather than an extramural dispute involving serious breaches of established biblical doctrine.

No one is a healer. I am not a healer. I would not be numbered among the charismatics. But I will pray for healing, because it is God alone who heals. Sometimes, especially in outpourings of the Spirit in awakenings, there are healings. Even in the Jesus People Movement some, but not all, were healed. We did not know why, nor could we predict outcomes, and we refused to blame the minister or the one who needed healing if there was no healing. Some were healed, however. That is my testimony. In the years since the Jesus People Movement, during what might be referred to as "normal times," compared to times of awakening, few are healed. Over the last three decades I have prayed for about twenty people, and to my knowledge not one was healed. Maybe it is better to be faithful, biblical, and hopeful than successful; in any case, in light of the current confusion and error regarding healing, I am beginning to reflect on my views and ministerial practices. Thus, I am considering including an opportunity for any who would like to have the elders of our church pray for them along the lines of James 5. If I do so, it will not make me a charismatic healer or a quack. And if a healing should occur, then to God be the glory. And if healing is not given, then to God be the glory.

January, 2010

Saints and Angels

Christians are worshipping saints and angels like never before—what's going on?

The worship or adoration of angels and saints is nothing new for Christians—it goes back many centuries. The Roman Catholic Church and the Eastern Orthodox Church both have extensive histories of honoring, adoring, and praying to angels and saints, the saints being purified believers now present with God in heaven. It is thought that each person has a guardian angel who is actively engaged in guidance and protection through granting answers to prayer and miraculous intervening in real time. Additionally, the purified and holy saints in heaven are considered able to interact with believers living today.

Though the Christian Scripture does not endorse or promote the worship of angels or saints, the traditions of these churches do, and they trump whatever proscriptions might be found in the Bible itself. Therefore, if the church sanctions angel and saint worship, then it is permitted for the individual believer.

The foregoing is well understood. However, some Protestants (maybe the term should rather be "neo-Protestants") are beginning to embrace the concept that angels and saints now in heaven are or should be involved in the life of the believer.

Bill Johnson, pastor of Bethel Church in Redding, California, wrote a book with the above title and believes that heaven has invaded earth by means of purified saints. Yes, he is not talking about the incarnation—the Word become flesh (see John 1:14) —he means that saints in "these last days" are engaged in empowering Christians to do mighty things, particularly healings.

It is all about power. A key phrase from Johnson is, "The kingdom of God is not a matter of talk but of power." As he describes it, saints, which are a part of the "mystical body of Christ in heaven," are eager to be joined with the "mystical body of Christ on earth," as in a marriage of a man and a woman. And when such a union occurs, then real kingdom power is unleashed and manifested with virtually unlimited scope and power. When this is realized, then the great branches of the Christian Church will be united.

Christians, Johnson teaches, may now avail themselves of the power of the Spirit, the angels, and the saints. He envisions the great cloud of saints in heaven becoming one with the believers on earth. Part of the authority for this doctrine comes from Hebrews 12:18-24 where in verses 22 and 23 are the words,

> "But you have come to Mount Zion and to the
> city of the living God, the heavenly Jerusalem,
> and to the assembly of the firstborn who are

enrolled in heaven, and to God, the judge of all, and to the spirits of the righteous made perfect." (ESV)

There is not space here to adequately expose the passage, but the interpretation that departed saints are eager to engage with believers on earth now and empower them is certainly unusual and has nothing in common with the vast majority of commentators and scholars. The general theme of the passage is that what God has done in Christ is to establish a kingdom that is complete and perfect and cannot be shaken or destroyed.

The great cloud of witnesses

The purified saints—the great cloud of witnesses— have been rewarded by God and given authority to intervene in or invade the affairs of Christians living today. The invaders have the ability to work great power miracles in the ministries of Christians who understand the empowerment and seek it. The Christian living today should seek this out, according to Johnson—this gifting, impartation, or anointing—and can then bring healing and words of knowledge or prophecy to the body of Christ on earth—very heady indeed.

Pastor Johnson of Bethel Church appeals to Matthew 10:41: "The one who receives a prophet because he is a prophet will receive a prophet's reward, and the one who receives a righteous person because he is a righteous person will receive a righteous person's reward." The context of the passage is plain enough. Jesus outlines the fact that those who will receive or hear the message of His representatives or followers are then receiving He Himself and will be rewarded with hearing the message of the Gospel. But Johnson makes the passage mean something else entirely. It is his way of encouraging Christians today to seek out the empowering of the "great cloud of witnesses"—the departed saints.

Johnson's warning

Bill Johnson certainly knows that his view is not broadly shared in the Christian community, so he therefore issues a warning. He understands that most biblically based Christians will have been taught that communicating with the saints in heaven is demonic in nature, that it is a deception perpetrated by the devil. The resultant fear of the devil's tricks, Johnson warns, would then cut one off from having faith in communion with the saints and the benefits available through the powerful working of these saints. A clever tactic indeed, bringing up and negating the argument Johnson knows will be used by biblically based Christians

Certainly, the Scripture is the barrier that Johnson must overcome. In chapter 6 of his book, Johnson concludes with this most revealing statement: "Those who feel safe because of their grasp of Scripture enjoy a false sense of security. We all have the Holy Spirit, but to follow Him, we must be willing to follow Him off the map—to go beyond what we know."

For Johnson it is not the Word of God but the new move of the "Spirit" that matters. It is all about power and not faithfulness to the Scripture. Christians who adhere to the Bible are then belittled as being stuck in old revelation and not able to follow the leading of the Spirit into new regions. So, let the Scripture go, follow the new anointing, receive the new impartations, be empowered by the purified saints.

Luke 16:26 nullifies Johnson's position

In the parable found in Luke 16:19-31, usually titled "The Rich Man and Lazarus," Jesus puts into Abraham's mouth a truth that clearly nullifies the theology behind Bill Johnson's idea that purified saints interact with living Christians. "'And besides all this, between us and you a great chasm has been fixed, in order that those who would pass from here to you may not be able, and none may cross from there to us'" (Luke 16:26).

Christians have long understood, based on such passages as Deuteronomy 18:9-14, that medium ship and necromancy are both forbidden by God and are abominable practices. Yet Bill Johnson celebrates such and encourages others to enter into this very thing. Of course, he does not frame it in occult terminology, but it is impossible to view it any other way. Yet, persons who claim Christ as Savior and hope to be biblically correct are falling into error on this point. One is reminded of a passage in Galatians where Paul referred to a moving away from Gospel truth into error, a "turning to a different gospel" (Galatians 1:6).

How did it come to this?

For people who have accepted the idea that God is doing new things in the "last days," any new direction is possible. Everything then appears to have changed, because the end is near, and it is by a display of power that the kingdom will come. Christians must then travel "off the map" if they really want to tap into what God is doing—and Johnson, among others, position themselves as direction-givers on that new map to tell us exactly what God is doing now. Amazingly, thousands believe this, and the numbers are growing. These concepts have exerted considerable influence not only in America, and not only among charismatics and Pentecostals, but in Latin American and in Africa. It is impossible to underestimate the influence of these ideas.

One note: How is it that one can be certain that the last days have come? Declarations that the end of history has come is nothing new. There is simply no way to know what God has determined by His own counsel.

Anyone can make a claim or utter a "prophecy," but experience and wisdom teach us that it is better to wait and see and not be pushed into adopting ideas that have a proven failure rate, which is 100%.

Why are these non-biblical ideas taking hold? Power, new anointing, new improved truth—the same old errors are at work once again. It is heady, it is powerful, for there is real power; miracles do happen—there is a real spirit at work, and when you see the power, you may well be convinced. What is crucial to understand here is that not all spiritual power is from God. The power gurus of Hinduism, like Osho or Muktananda, performed amazing power miracles. Power is deceptive. The magicians of Egypt were temporarily able to imitate the power of God demonstrated through Moses.

Are those who propound communion with departed saints in order to acquire their power evil persons bent on misleading the people of God? Not necessarily. But, demonic deception and human error are both real.

Angel of light

In the church at Corinth Paul realized there were men who had a ministry that was running counter to that which he had been commissioned by Christ to preach. From the reports that Paul had received he understood the dangers involved. Here is how Paul described the situation:

> For such men are false apostles, deceitful workmen, disguising themselves as apostles of Christ. And no wonder, for even Satan disguises himself as an angel of light. So it is no surprise if his servants also disguise themselves as servants of righteousness.
> 2 Corinthians 11:13-15

"Angel of light"—who would not be deceived, especially if one thought that the last days had come and everything had changed and we were "off the map"? With angels of light you can imagine there would be amazing knowledge and power. It may be that those who are sure they cannot be tricked are most vulnerable to being tricked.

Summary and conclusion

Realizing the need to write this has not been pleasant, but as a pastor I am obligated to warn and protect the flock God has given me. I intend this also for a wider audience, because our part of the world has already been impacted by the false teaching described in this article.

We are not to be united with departed and perfected saints in heaven. As born-again followers of Jesus, we are indwelt by the Holy Spirit and have the written Word of God to instruct us. We have all we need. And God will bring in His Kingdom in His own time.

To be clear about this, my conviction is that communication with so-called saints in heaven is actually trafficking with demons. It is a base deception to suggest that Christians are to seek empowerment from the saints in heaven.

We are not to seek out departed saints or pray to or worship angels (see Colossians 2:16-20. In addition recall that when Jesus taught His disciples to pray the key words were "Our Father in heaven" and not an "Our angel" or "Our saint") No, we are to be faithful followers of Jesus who are already empowered with the Spirit to proclaim the Good News of the cross and resurrection. This is our work, whether Jesus will return for us tomorrow or in a thousand years.

November, 2009

My years as a tongues speaker

Some background:

This is the first in a series on my life as a flaming Pentecostal; well maybe not so much flaming as in Holy Roller, but my life in the Charismatic/Pentecostal fold. It all began, strangely enough, in Portland, Oregon with what happened down at the local Odd Fellows Hall.

Two blocks from the family home in Northeast Portland, on Deacon and Durham Street, was the Odd Fellows Hall, which was rented out by different groups. It no longer exists, and probably the huge old wooden, two-story structure burned down. When Pentecostal meetings were sweeping Portland, one met there, and it was wild. My brothers and I plus a kid named Topsy would sneak in and watch. We slipped in the back doors, found seats in the back, and got our entertainment. Since that day I have never seen anything quite like it. There was actual rolling around on the floor. My dad said nothing too bad but nothing too good about it all. I don't know that he ever went in there, but he definitely went to the North Baptist Church about a mile from the house.

My dad had not yet become a Christian, a real one I mean, and I think he attended church out of tradition, because his folks were the quiet, serious kind of Baptists.

I'll jump now to 1963 and the First Baptist Church of Fairfield, California and my conversion at age 21. I will not walk us through it here, but after a period of nine months of sporadic listening to the Gospel preached by Pastor Bob Lewis, I experienced the new birth. It is still mostly a mystery to me. Pastor Bob was in his mid-thirties and was serious about discipleship. A book he gave to all of us new believers was on the Bible-based American cults. It was a small volume and discussed only five such groups: Mormons, Jehovah Witnesses, Christian Science, Adventists (Seventh Day), and Pentecostals.

Back then Pentecostals were rightfully included in such a book, but today that is not the case. Most people do not understand that in the early years of the 20th century Pentecostals earned the designation of "cult," because they believed that they were the only ones really filled with the Holy Spirit and that speaking in tongues was the only sure mark of a real born-again Christian. This took them into the cultic realm.

So then, reading that book I was convinced that Pentecostals were cultic, and I gave them and their doctrines wide berth. This was my mind set all the way to 1968 and the Jesus People Movement.

September, 2012

Am I Pentecostal?

My sermon for the last Sunday of May was entitled A safe place. The sermon for the first Sunday of June was "I am Pentecostal." The one explains the other. Or, to put it another way, because I am pentecostal (no capital P) there is a good chance that the church will be a safe place for people to be converted and grow up into the fullness of Jesus Christ.

If preachers are dependent on the Holy Spirit of God to do the work of conversion, they are less likely to resort to methods, techniques, and strategies to get people to make a decision to become a Christian (the devil, they say, is in the details—and he certainly gets into these methodology details!)

When all else is left aside, no matter how relevant or trendy it might seem, the simple gospel of Jesus Christ, comprising both law and grace, can be presented to all who will hear, and then it is the Holy Spirit who will convict of sin and reveal Jesus and his cross and resurrection.

The preacher must therefore be pentecostal—one who looks to the Holy Spirit to do his work. Otherwise, we will be strongly tempted to 'assist' in the process of regeneration—with the potential result of false conversions.

Anxious parents

This perspective affects every aspect of church life. Consider church discipline. If a pastor depends on the Spirit of God to grow people into the fullness of Christ, then he is less likely to meddle unnecessarily in that process. He will not attempt to force growth or raise expectations beyond normal levels of maturity in dealing with the babes, children, youth, and elders in the church.

Anxious parents, especially those who are overly concerned with appearances and performance, can easily discourage their immature children or even incite rebellion in them. A failure to understand that different Christians grow spiritually at different rates can create an unsafe church environment.

Before my conversion I was a UFO fan and mentioned this to several people at the church I was attending. Fortunately, no one tried to correct me! If they had, I might have walked away.

I have sometimes offended unbelievers by trying to bring them into line with my way of thinking (biblical though it was) instead of simply presenting the doctrines of grace. In addition, I have sometimes been guilty of trying to make spiritual adults out of mere infants in Christ—shoving strong meat at them instead of milk.

Pastoral caring

What I have written above does not come easily to me as a pastor. There are times when I would love to reprove people for the sub-biblical doctrine they are holding onto, or to correct behavior that doesn't match standard New Testament ethics.

Frankly, I love to advise and counsel, which is fine, if such is sought. But I have a tendency to be impatient and overly forward. Times when I thought I was helping, it turned out to be the opposite.

My pastoral caring looks different now that I am past my fifth decade of ministry. It is not that I have gotten old and lazy. Old maybe, but not lazy—I work harder now than I ever did (see Colossians 1:29). But I am trusting more in the ministry of the Holy Spirit and depending less on my own zeal and wisdom.

I am convinced that the divine Parent who brings a son or daughter into the world is best able to grow that precious child into exactly what he wants that child to be.

So, yes, I am pentecostal (with no capital P).

September, 2013

A Critical Analysis of the New Apostolic Reformation

The New Apostolic Reformation (NAR) is not an organization but a relational alignment of churches and groups that voluntarily connect with recognized apostles and prophets. C. Peter Wagner, former professor at Fuller Theological Seminary in Pasadena, California, now deceased, began using the title in 2000 or 2001. A partial listing of leaders typically associated with the NAR is Che Ahn, John and Carol Arnott, Heidi (and Roland) Baker, Mike Bickle of IHOP in Kansas City, Stacey Campbell, Randy Clark, James Goll, Cindy Jacobs, Rick Joyner of Morningstar in South Carolina, Bill Johnson and Kris Vallotton of the Bethel Church in Redding, California, Patricia King, Chuck D. Pierce, Dutch and Tim Sheets, and Brian Simmons (the Passion Translation).

A major aspect of this so-called reformation is the establishment of the "Fivefold ministry" as we find it in Ephesians 4:11—apostles, prophets, evangelists, pastors and teachers. However, the NAR emphasizes apostles and prophets, the prophets declaring what God is doing and the apostles making it work out in real time.

Perhaps the most alarming aspect of the NAR is the development of a "we-they" cultic mindset. Some prophets have announced that a "Christian civil war" is even now being waged, spiritual in nature but potentially physical.

America and the New Apostolic Reformation

It is evident to most American Christians that in our current culture there is a decided tilt away from the Christian and Biblical moorings which marked previous generations. This is seen is the continuing acceptance of same-sex marriage and all forms of gender and sexual identity, little concern about abortion, and a growing acceptance of the drug culture—among other markers of a deteriorating society.

In California, along with a number of other states, marijuana use is legal and some of my neighbors, here in upscale Marin County, grow the weed. I have daily read the San Francisco Chronicle and the Marin Independent Journal since 1965—and my observation is we are living in a "stoner" world that makes the hippie scene of the late 1960s look tame. Every day in the San Francisco Bay Area people are robbed, mugged, raped, and murdered by addicts of one kind or another. We are now living in a dangerous world, and speaking out against it is definitely politically incorrect. Hard to imagine!

Christians, perhaps more readily than others, are aware that as a nation we are going to hell in the proverbial hand basket. What to do? Well, we preach, we pray, we witness, and we lobby as best we can, but the slippery slope just becomes steeper and steeper.

I have noticed that some Christian organizations that are not aligned with the New Apostolic Reformation and would not even embrace NAR's core theology, nevertheless cooperate to certain degrees in NAR-organized conferences and alliances. (I have in mind here Focus on the Family and Cru.) The question then is: If there are major differences in worldviews, why the entanglement?

My suspicion is that NAR leaders and organizations hold that God is establishing the kingdom of God on earth right now, at least in America. The seven mountains encompass, among others, the family, education, and government, and thus the effort to bring major politicians into the movement. Some of the names mentioned by NAR people are Sarah Palin, Ted Cruz, Rick Perry, even President Trump. Of course, politicians need a voter base, and evangelicals are one of the largest, but I personally do not include myself in anyone's voter base.

A Connection with Islam

The NAR is both political and religious, much like Islam

is. The goal of Islam is to see Sharia Law extended globally. Islam does not distinguish between politics and religion; for Muslims the two are wed.

Islam does not cherish the separation of church and state. I have read the same in some of the NAR writings. Clearly, the goal is to see the Kingdom rule over the globe, especially and foremost in American, and this does not mean the conversion of everyone to Christ. There is talk of a "Christian civil war,"[1] and with some writers it appears as though things could get violent.

Where Islam already dominates, it is enough that non-believers submit themselves to Muslim authority; the alternative is death. It is join, submit, or die. Islam says this is what brings peace, which underlies what is meant by Islam being the religion of peace. Does NAR, or some portion thereof, have a counterpart view?

NAR people believe God will establish His rule when the offices of apostle and prophet are again in place and when the mountain of government is dominated through the apostolic and prophetic authority. That sets the stage for the coming of the Kingdom, and Jesus descends from heaven.

The above view is termed dominionism. Simply put, the Church dominates, and everything is under its

---

[1] On one side are those aligned with NAR apostles and prophets and on the other are those "opposers" who are not, people like me.

authority. America is pristine once again. Then the world follows. Heaven then is not an eternal fellowship with God in His presence but is a rule over the world. Heaven may follow, but not before dominion.

The Mission of the Church

We are not called to rule; we are called to witness. We are to make disciples of all nations. We preach Jesus and teach new believers, starting with baptizing them in the name of the Father, and of the Son, and of the Holy Spirit. Plain enough. The Holy Spirit equips us to do all this (see Matthew 28:18-20 and Acts 1:1-8).

Jesus will return and establish His kingdom exactly when He chooses. Once again, plain and simple. This is Biblical Christianity. NAR's agenda is unbiblical and thus is sub-Christian.

Is this an unfair or inaccurate evaluation?

Why We Must Oppose the New Apostolic Reformation

In 1965, I started pastoring churches in the greater San Francisco Bay Area. I quickly learned that a primary aspect of the work of a pastor is to protect the flock against all that threatens it.

Since 1984, I have led Miller Avenue Baptist Church in Mill Valley, California, and I have become increasingly aware of the dangers posed by what is widely known as The New Apostolic Reformation. At first, I merely noted it and followed it to some degree but was not motivated to directly speak out against it except for writing an essay or two about certain practices associated with it. A number of these can be found in section two.

Recently, a member of our congregation asked what I thought about a book written by Bill Johnson, one of the top names in the movement and lead pastor of Bethel Church in Redding, California. This woke me up finally, and to make a long story short, I knew it was now time to tend to the sheep's safety.

The tremendous growth and influence of the New Apostolic Reformation (here out the NAR) is shocking, and I was rather unaware of how extensively the movement has taken hold all over the world, with a very large presence in Asia, Africa, and Latin America, as well as having advanced significantly in North America. What could and should I do?

A Civil War?

Some NAR apostles and prophets are speaking of a civil war being currently fought within Christianity. NAR advocates seem surprised that not all Christians are jumping on board the "final movement," which they are sure will usher in the kingdom of God in these last days. However, many are contesting the NAR; I am only one in a long line of Christians to question them.

Another reason for my opposition to the NAR apostles and prophets is the tendency for individuals and organizations so identified to say and do wild and crazy things that can only be called an embarrassment to Biblical Christianity. Most non-Christians are not able to discern the differences within Christianity and see even the Bible-based cults like Mormonism and Jehovah's Witnesses as belonging to mainstream Christianity. The offense of the Gospel is obstacle enough, but the absurd nature of proclamations made by the NAR-aligned prophets and apostles is beyond offensive.

Mainstream media has largely ignored the antics of the NAR folk, though a few reports of weird happenings get out, and the bizarre nature of the events and claims are interesting enough to spark more interest. I predict that awareness of NAR activities will increase. Some film crew is bound to do a documentary on it that will be embraced by the secular community as representative of what the Christians are up to now. And then Christians and Christianity will be made to look more foolish than it already is in the minds of many.

We Christians are indeed divided about this, and necessarily so. Soon after this book is published, my next project focuses on that which unites Christians, whether they be Catholic, Eastern Orthodox, Protestant, Messianic, or charismatic/Pentecostal: Biblical Christianity is Evangelical, and this is the working title for the new book. By "evangelical," I mean that all Christians are given the commission by Jesus Himself to be witness of His saving grace to the entire world. The primary objective of evangelical Christianity is not to take over the world, known as dominionism, but to present Jesus and His finished work on the cross to the world.

What is my standing?

Do I have a right or platform to speak out on the NAR in the first place? I think I do have the right and the obligation that comes with being a pastor. But I have additional background that gives me the experience and understanding of what this movement can perpetrate.

When I was twenty-one years old, mid-way through a four-year enlistment in the Air Force, I became a follower of Jesus Christ. This was in 1963. After my discharge from the military (having served as a medic) I moved to the campus of Golden Gate Baptist Theological Seminary in Mill Valley, California. During two and a half years of my student term I pastored the Excelsior Baptist Church in Byron, California. Also, beginning in February of 1967, I engaged in "street ministry" in the Haight-Ashbury District of San Francisco, leading to my involvement in the Jesus People Movement from 1967 to 1972. Around the middle of that time period I was plunged full force into the charismatic/Pentecostal movement. Yes, in 1968 I woke up one morning speaking loudly in tongues and became engaged with the charismania sprouting up everywhere.

Despite my being a faithful Southern Baptist, I became rather "wild-eyed," as we used to say. I was also much engaged with Catholic charismatics, attended and even spoke at Full Gospel Businessmen meetings, and participated in other charismatic events. Lonnie Frisbee was a close friend, and when he requested my opinion, I urged him to unite with Chuck Smith and the beginnings of the Calvary Chapel days in Costa Mesa, California.

My Jesus People ministry focused on the San Francisco Bay Area where we established house churches, bookstores, high school and college ministries, and much more. I completed a MDiv degree in 1969 and went on to do a ThM, both at Golden Gate Seminary. However, the seminary refused to award the ThM degree, because I was a tongues speaker. (My major professor finally told me this was the reason for the continued rejection of my thesis, A Manual of Demonology and the Occult, which Zondervan did publish in 1973.)

While mid-point in a DMin degree program at San Francisco Theological Seminary, my major professor told me that the church I pastored was not healthy, which shocked me beyond words. The very next week I brought him a copy of our doctrinal statement. His response was that we were theologically orthodox enough, but our methodology, our ecclesiology, was errant.

I had little choice other than to take this acknowledged authority on cults and conversion seriously. It was a "dark night of the soul" experience. Without intending to do so, I isolated myself from nearly all the other pastors and elders in our little community of churches that stretched from Sonoma to San Jose. Slowly, ever so slowly, I began to see what the professor said was true. I will give only one keen example of what I realized was error about the way we did our ministry.

At a memorial service

In 1980 I resigned my position as pastor of the church in San Rafael, California. I went to law school, figured out a way to make a living, partially lost my family, declared bankruptcy, and nearly walked away from anything involving Christianity. (This reactionary response lasted two weeks.)

At some point, I do not recall the date, I attended a memorial service for the son of one of the pastors in our community of churches. During the gathering after the service I was accosted by a woman who had been part of the San Rafael church during the 1970s. In front of hundreds of people, she shouted out how I was to blame for her marrying the man with whom she had two children, both of whom her husband had molested, crimes for which he was presently serving a long prison sentence. She screamed that had I forced her to do so by means of a prophecy that she must marry the young man with whom she had been fornicating. She had little choice than to do what I had "heard from the Lord."

The point here is that I had thought it was entirely suitable to ask God to "give me a word" and then prophesy over people. We directed people to do what came to us by impressions, by whatever came into our minds, which was usually what the elders and pastors had already decided should be done. We thought nothing of it and had no idea that we were manipulating people—thus our faulty, cultic methodology. My professor was correct in his evaluation.

References to "charismatic/Pentecostalism"

Please understand that I am not attacking those who are charismatic and/or Pentecostal, but the reality is that much of the NAR emerged out of the charismatic and Pentecostal movement. And today I find that the churches and groups that identify as charismatic/Pentecostal are more open to the ideologies of the NAR.

Recovery from the cultic mentality

That is how it began for me. For the first time I recognized that I needed recovery every bit as much as any addict. I had suffered loss—my position as pastor, my wife, a family identity, and so much more. Later on, when I was once again a pastor, now at Miller Avenue Baptist Church, I developed a program designed to help people recover from their involvement in cultic groups. Over the course of six years I facilitated twelve sessions, each one lasting twenty-three weeks. We had ex-Mormons, Jehovah's Witnesses, and primarily former members of the church I had pastored in the 1970s, plus others. Those who attended faced up to what they had lost, and it was painful, very painful to take a close look at what had happened to them and what they had done to others. It is still uncomfortable for me to think about.

My point is that many of those who have been and

are yet to be involved in the NAR will need recovery, because it will and must come to an end. Evidence points to the fact that it is imploding from the inside out. And those effected are precious brothers and sisters in Christ. Some may be tempted to suicide, some perhaps to revenge, and most will be emotionally devastated. Many will simply want to walk away from anything Christian, thinking they had merely been duped and used.

I do not intend to bring grief to the Christian family. In speaking out and opposing the NAR I hope to bring peace and healing. Naming names and pointing out blatant error is not mean-spirited; it is what both Jesus and the New Testament authors did regularly. There are counterfeits, there are demons teaching error, there are false apostles and prophets. To leave it all unchallenged is unbiblical and unChristian.

Many are now leaving churches that have an NAR alignment or affiliation. You will find stories of those who have left NAR churches at http://bereanresearch.org.

The Devil's Greatest Achievements

That old devil has been incredibly successful of late. Let me count the ways:

God haters

Perhaps heading the list is the fact that most non-Christians lump all the branches, denominations, sects, cults, and crazy little offshoots of Christianity into the same grimy and cruddy bag. It's convenient, of course, for those who are God haters.

Am I being too harsh with this language? I mean, "God haters." Is this fair?

Maybe not exactly fair, but it might well be accurate. What I mean is, there is a hatred of the God of the Christians as expressed in our Bible, because this is a sin-hating God. And why would God hate sin? We Christians know the answer to this question: it is because sin destroys us, little by little. And few understand or acknowledge how it works.

Just what is a Christian?

Here is a brief pause for a little theology. What in the world is a Christian, anyway?

Starting from the negative, it is not simply someone who is a member of a church. Nor is it someone who has been baptized, nor someone who is squeaky clean and helps others, even a lot. Now from the positive, it is someone who has been convicted that he or she is lost and without hope but who has an interest in Jesus. This is how it starts. Then, in a way no one can explain, the Holy Spirit of God brings the new birth.

Some readers have never heard of such a thing. If that is true of you, read the third chapter of John's Gospel. Clear as a bell.

All Christians are now scandalized

One might be a member of the Roman Catholic Church and be a Christian. Okay, one might be a member of the church I pastor and may not be a Christian. Look at any church group, and within can be found real born-again believers, or maybe not. My guess is that the more evangelical the core message is, the greater the chance of people being the real deal, since the message of Jesus, His life, death, resurrection, and so on, is what defines an evangelical gathering—that is, unless they have gone soft on the Gospel in an effort to be more "seeker friendly."

Here is the secret: there is a visible and an invisible church. The invisible Church is known only to God. When we all get to heaven, some of us straight-laced, fundamental types will be aghast to find Russian Orthodox, Old Latin Catholics, Pentecostals even, perhaps a Baptist or two, huddled around the throne of God shouting "hallelujah." Shocking I know, but this notion is solid biblical Christian doctrine.

It is the visible church that is run by and seen by humans. This church runs for cover whenever challenged by the culture.

So, do I think things will change much regarding the liberalization of the modern Western church? Maybe not for a while, but once the depth of degradation becomes widely revealed, stories that will curl your toes, about the ravages of sin held up for all to view—there will be some reversal of course. There will be those who wish we hadn't taken homosexual behavior mainline, taken pride in it, and celebrated it. Will the highly successful promo, "If you haven't tried it, don't knock it," wear thin when the full and ripe fruit appears?

Hocus-Pocus Magic

Let's move on. I am thinking of magic in the church. And yes, there has been a tendency to that for millennia. The priest waves over the offertory and chants a "hocus pocus,"[1] and some flat bread and cheap wine becoming the body and blood of Jesus. Billions have believed this!

---

[1] This is Latin for what was actually uttered by the priest in this ritual.

More magic: water sprinkled on the forehead of an infant, and shazam, all the dirty old sin of Adam that penetrated the baby at conception is suddenly gone with the word of the priest/magician. You will not find that one in the Bible!

I see it as a power play foisted upon folks a long time ago to consolidate power and authority. It worked for about 1,000 years; then came a protest, and Protestants emerged. Are you shocked to see it this way? It is no sin to think things through.

The demonic business model

Something else: the church as corporation. This is one of my pet peeves. Grand structures, fancy religious clothing replete with pointed hats and brightly colored flowing robes. Supposedly, with all the marvelous cathedrals and vestments, it must be of God. But the common sinners must confess and bow down in obeisance, cowering in awe but not in happy awe. They must worry that every sin takes away the temporary salvation they received at the last mass. So, money offerings become a way to salve the conscience.

The church as a business, tax exempt, issuing tax deductible receipts, non-profit status, preachers getting tax breaks, committees, councils, boards, corporate, retirement and health benefits. Maybe even a parsonage, manse, rectory, parish house to live in.

There is more, or maybe I have gone overboard, but where is the Church of the Book of Acts? Where is the Bold Proclamation of the Gospel these days?

Bold proclamation of the Gospel

My congregation and I happen to be a small part of a new trend in the ways and means of evangelism. Christians all over the world are leveraging the technological era. Not only is this going on globally, it is spurred by the Holy Spirit who is highly skilled at using the Internet and all other forms of media.

Perhaps we are in the midst of a new awakening, and if this is so, then it is the fifth awakening in America's history. Since we (I, wife Katie, and the folk at Miller Avenue Baptist Church) have been publishing books and producing television programs, along with attending the International Christian Retail Show and the National Religious Broadcasters conventions, we encounter Christians and their organizations from all over the world. I can testify that the proclamation is becoming bold and smart. The message of Jesus gets into even the small cracks, where the Gospel has not penetrated before. Movies, television, online videos, live streaming, websites, blogs, radio, podcasts, and more are the now usual platforms for the message of Jesus. Even, try as they might, the Muslim clerics are not able to keep the testimony of Jesus out of the eyes and hears of young Muslims. This cannot be stopped unless a catastrophic event occurs that pushes us back into the Stone Age.

It is like the days of the Jesus People Movement, with Christians' street preaching, playing gospel music, and witnessing in the streets, we now have many streets—those made of asphalt and those made of electronic pulses. Never before, in my estimation, have we been harder at work doing what Jesus said to do, "Go into all the world."

Faith or feelings?

Lastly, and this may derail much of the good news about internet evangelism, is the confusing of faith with feelings. This may be the devil's greatest achievement, his most pernicious scheme of all.

Beware, this is subtle and difficult to describe.

The band, the band, the band! It's all about the music, the beat, the swaying and hand raising, the drone of minimal lyrics. The devil does not have all the good music. "Good music" is in our old hymn books and with some of the recent generation of song writers who write really good tunes along with rock hard Bible truth. However, way too much of what passes today as worship is aimed at getting our feelings aroused and massaged.

Can anyone point to a time when people were living in

such a high state of anxiety? Is this the "Age of anxiety" as many claim?

I feel it. I am alternately sad and glad. Sad due to world and national events, glad because my team won yesterday. (Not an even tradeoff.)

We need help and there is plenty of it out there, and the church is contributing, but so very often in ways that are, in the long run, destructive.

Back to the band. I had one, Joyful Noise, from 1968 to 1972, and it was wonderful folk-like Jesus music. Then the pros got ahold of it, and we moved toward music designed to get crowds pumped up and wild with hallelujahs. Falling out, going down under the power, dancing wildly, blindly, by the hour. But it felt good!

Entertainment is a huge part of our daily lives today; we love to be entertained. It makes us feel good. The band is front and center on the stage, drums prominent, with flashing lights, an extravagant sound system, double screens displaying videos, lyrics, and slides, and the worship time, the ministry time, prophetic words bouncing off the walls, almost a weeping and gnashing of teeth.

And we call this feel-good-faith, because faith has been confused with feelings.

Forgiveness is not a feeling; it is a faith act, a faith fact. I may be miserable but be trusting in Jesus that His shed blood covers my sin, and all of it, past, present, and future. Do I have to be glad? Can't I be sad when I see my sin? Joy follows the reality of the promise of total forgiveness, and joy is not a feeling, either. Joy is beyond feeling, above feeling, sideways of feeling; it is not to be compared. It is being in the glory of the presence of God, this joy inexpressible. I can be in a prison cell during the middle of the night and during a storm, yet still have joy.

I would prefer that instead of the worship leader (is there such a thing in Scripture?) leading cheers, we hear about how and why all our sin has been placed on our Lord Jesus on the cross, and that sin being buried, gone forever. Then I can come in confession for my recent sins and know I am covered.

What our world needs is not more music, not larger screens in front of the auditorium or the latest in audio boards; we need solid Bible teaching and preaching.

The devil has had his (its) day. Now comes the bold proclamation of the Gospel.

Now, also, comes an advertisement: We, my wife Katie and I, have other "Little Books" out: *Biblical Christianity is Evangelical*, *The Preposterous God*, *Spiritual Health*, and *What's So Bad about Hell?* You can get these through Amazon.com or ask your local bookstore to order them from Ingram. We are hoping you will use them as tracts to give to others, either by buying several (priced low for the purpose) or by reading them then giving them away. That is a way to reflect the times when we directly handed out Gospel material to others. You too can be a direct and personal witness for Christ.

Let me close with this: If you follow through with this direct and bold proclamation of the Gospel you will be entering into the grand and great adventure, living like the Book of Acts brothers and sisters. You will never be the same.

Try it, you will like it.

October, 2018

Christian Mystics?

What is a mystic? The *Oxford Concise English Dictionary*, published by Oxford Press, tells us: Mystic – "a person who seeks by contemplation and self-surrender to obtain unity or identity with or absorption into the Deity or the ultimate reality, or who believes in the spiritual apprehension of truths that are beyond the understanding."

On this definition we can agree. The mystic, the shaman, the Santerían priest or priestess, Wiccan, medium, channeller, psychic, yogi—they all rely on the soul journey while in an ecstasy or trance state to gain special knowledge or experience. A survey of the techniques employed by various religious traditions used to reach the trance state include deep breathing, centering, meditation, tobacco juice, peyote, mescaline, drumming, dancing, and often these in combination. In the ecstasy or trance, entities, animal spirits, fairies, elves, demons, angels, gods, goddesses, and the list goes on, show up to guide the person on the soul journey.

But what about the *Christian* mystic? Is it normative and biblical for Christians to rely upon a trance state in order to obtain experience with God? There are those in the broad Christian community who will answer yes to this question, and here I am thinking of those who practice "contemplative prayer" and hold up Theresa of Avila, St. John of the Cross, St. Ignatius of Loyola, and others, as worthy examples. For these noted Christian mystics of the past, the goal was to experience God, the very presence of God, and communicate directly with angels, saints, even Jesus.

Advocates of contemplative prayer or deep meditation suggest the following to enter into an ecstasy so that there may be an experience with Deity: Find a place alone and apart, be comfortable, calm yourself, center and ground, light a candle, breathe slowly and rhythmically, focus on the name of God or visualize Jesus, Mary, or a saint, empty the mind, focus, and open the mind and heart to whatever God will give to you.

It might be worth asking whether this is at all biblical, and for some the answer runs close to, "We may not find such instruction in the Bible, but it is not unbiblical."

Unbiblical? This is a serious question, since there are so many who center and depend upon the trance state and who are nowhere close to being either biblical or Christian. I have in mind the shaman, the witch, the priests and priestesses of Santería and Vodun (Voodoo), even those who openly worship Satan. These spiritual practices are to be strenuously avoided by the Christian.

The culture always reacts against the authority given

to the Bible; most all Christians experience this to one degree or another, often as rejection of them or their beliefs. The alternative, however, is not reassuring, as cultural values come and go like the wind. Generally, people want to sanction what they want to do and what makes them feel good. But this puts us on shaky ground or the proverbial slippery slope. The Scripture, on the other hand, is tried in the fire and not found wanting. Great nations and peoples have been built on its foundation, while those who ignore and reject the Word of God have historically not fared well. And ultimately, it is the believer's direct encounter with the Bible that is determinative.

Biblically speaking, it is clear that Satan disguises himself as an angel of light (see 2 Corinthians 11:14–15). In addition, Jesus warned that toward the end of history and just before the Day of Judgment "false christs and false prophets will arise and perform great signs and wonders, so as to lead astray, if possible, even the elect" (Matthew 24:24). And perhaps the most stunning warning is Paul's: "The coming of the lawless one is by the activity of Satan with all power and false signs and wonders, and with all wicked deception for those who are perishing, because they refused to love the truth and so be saved" (2 Thessalonians 2:9-10).

How difficult it is to evaluate spiritual experiences! We tend to be accepting of them due to their awe-inspiring nature. Yet, the wise Christian needs to be assured that whatever spiritual practices are engaged in have both biblical precedent and warrant.

The Genuine Christian Mystic

The purpose of this essay is to point out something that has been known to Christians of all varieties down through the centuries: there is indeed a Christian mysticism that has both biblical precedent and warrant. By precedent I mean something that is already observed and practiced in Scripture. Prayer and meditation, which are mindful, alert, and conscious, are focused on God, both who He is and what He has done. This is beyond dispute. An established precedent is that the people of God, whether seen in the New or Old Testament, prayed to and thought intensely and seriously about God.

Warrant is that which is taught—not just observed—in Scripture, and prayer and meditation are taught and encouraged by, among others, David, Jesus, Paul, and John. With these then in place, precedence and warrant, prayer and meditation enjoy full biblical authority for all those in Christ who desire to seek union and deep fellowship with the Triune God.

Every person who is born from above, called born again, is indwelt by the Holy Spirit. Imagine that the Father, Son, and Holy Spirit indwell the believer as He dwelt in the Holy of Holies in the Temple in Jerusalem.

This Holy Spirit "bears witness with our spirit that we are children of God" (Romans 8:16). Here it is: The Holy Spirit who indwells each believer will bring to our remembrance the things that Jesus has said, as we find recorded in the New Testament (see John 14:26).

It is therefore clear that the Christian "mystic" does not depend on a trance state or ecstasy to achieve experience or knowledge of God. (By the way, nowhere in Scripture is there an instruction to "experience" God, and no one in Scripture set out to do so. In addition, it would not be biblical to refer to oneself as a mystic, since such a designation is not found in Scripture.)

The Spirit indwelt Christian then has the experience of God in at least two ways: one, in prayer, and two, in reading the Scripture, and the efficacy of both are dependent on the inner working and witness of the Holy Spirit. Neither prayer nor meditation involve an ecstasy or trance state.

In bringing our cares, requests, and words of praise and worship to God as we are encouraged to do, we are in the very presence of God, since we are "seated" or resting with Jesus at the right hand of God the Father. Not only that, but as we study the Scripture, God reveals Himself to us as we do so. It is a most amazing experience and has meant so much to me personally.

It has been my great pleasure and privilege to be a teacher and preacher of the Gospel for close to fifty years now. These responsibilities have brought me into a study of the Bible that I would probably not have known otherwise. How many dozens of times, perhaps hundreds of times, have I recognized the windows of heaven open, and in a most conscious and alert state of mind have I experienced God, personally and directly. I was not seeking such, but this would happen. I do not have the words to describe it, but the "ah ha" moments almost always involve something I have learned about Jesus and His grace extended toward me. Whatever I take away from these experiences is always in harmony with mainstream and historic Christianity. Maybe I could boil it down to this: the Holy Spirit showed me more of Jesus.

Am I a Christian mystic? No, I am an ordinary follower and servant of Jesus, probably more unspiritual than many, as I have always struggled with prayer, but none-theless, I do experience or encounter God in prayer and Bible study. I am satisfied in my innermost being, all the while living the life of a very busy, often stressed-out person in a crazy world.

Talking to an Angel

Talking to an angel is a favorite claim made by witches and priests and priestesses of shamanistic religions like Santería, and it is also being engaged in more and more by those claiming the Christian label who are associated with "Charisma."

Many will not know the name of William Branham, a faith healer active in the mid-twentieth century in America. He had an invisible angel, Emily by name, who stood beside him and whispered in his ear information such as the location and physical ailments of people in the audience. Branham would call out their names, accompanied by ohs and ahs from the audience, and they would be called forward and healed or healed where they sat. Whether there was actual healing or not is a tough call to make. Then along came Todd Bentley who did the same, even aided by the same angel that stood alongside Branham, but Bentley called the angel Emy.

There is currently much more of this happening for some time, as will be evident in an email I received yesterday from a person living in England. I give you now the raw and unedited email.

Dear Sir,

I am writing to thank you for the articles on your website which I have revisited a number of times, particularly the articles on the Toronto Blessing & related subjects. I am from Bath in the UK where I have lived for 44 years but am deeply troubled by the deception that has been emerging here for several decades, some of it so dangerous that I am praying about moving away as it is so seductive and hard to resist and one can feel a strong pull back because of decades of association with Christians friends who are still involved. Bath is a major tourist city which attracts large numbers of visitors from all over the world and I am not surprised to find such a city of influence in such a battle against false teaching. The Toronto "experience" (and associated moves & network of ministries) has taken such a strong hold here that it has been an enormous struggle disentangling from it - indeed I still have days my mind feels extremely confused. "River Revival" leaders are regularly invited here and Bath hosts the HQs of 2 major Word of Faith teachers. Recently I had to leave my fellowship because of a growing preoccupation with angels: one of the leaders regularly "sees angels" and reports to the congregation what they are saying to him/them and doing in the meeting, and on one occasion he prayed for the whole congregation to have visitations of angels; he has also started a "school of seer" to encourage similar encounters, and some of the other members are also "seeing angels". Most of the teaching comes in the form of "words" or "prophecies" or dreams, the little bible teaching is usually interpreted in an allegorical fashion to prop up their theology and usually on the same theme. The final straw was the outbreak of very bizarre & disturbing behavior in a Sunday meeting in early June which gave me such a severe panic attack, I never went back, as I am afraid of having them lay hands on me and impart something demonic. It was as if the Lord suddenly opened my eyes to see what was really going on. After much prayer I have since emailed them to express my concerns about Toronto and the dangers of seeking angelic encounters and continuing to pray for them and seeking the Lord as to what to do next. It has really helped me to find websites and articles such as yours with useful insight and teaching about these issues, and reassured me that I am (hopefully) not totally backsliding or going crazy but hearing the Lord warn me; I thank the Lord He is leading me to others in the Body of Christ around the world via the internet who are sharing the discernment and knowledge He has given them and to know I am not alone in this. Thank you for your time and efforts in making these articles available. May the Lord bless you and those you fellowship with and keep you on the right road.

Kind regards, England

The phenomenon of people talking to angels was to be expected. For instance, the steady stream of supposedly miraculous events at Bethel, IHOP, Toronto's Catch the Fire, and Morning Star were bound to wear out and become common place. Gold tooth fillings, feathers floating around, gold dust swirling in glory clouds, resurrections from the dead (reported but not documented by outsiders), and other wild stuff—there had to be more.

Consider angels for a moment. There was Mohammed who conversed with Gabriel, or so he thought, and the result was the Koran (Quran). Then Joseph Smith and the angel Moroni who provided the golden tablets, that when translated became the Book of Mormon. Of course, more recently we have had the Course in Miracles, but this time not an angel but Jesus Himself was supposedly the source. And how many other religions had their beginnings with an angelic visitation?

Angels are awe-inspiring; they can even appear as angels of light. Paul's warning in 2 Corinthians 11:12-15 is extremely relevant for us right now.

And the problem is exacerbated, because reports of

conversations with angels are made by important leaders. If any questions are raised about the authenticity of the event and/or message, it would likely mean risking one's status or even membership in whatever group or church was involved.

The angel phenomenon will not go away in the near future, but two questions remain. One, what comes next when the angel craze fades? and two, what harm will be done to those who are under the spell of the charismatic/Pentecostal guru who claims to be conversing with the heavenlies?

February, 2013

www.ingramcontent.com/pod-product-compliance
Lightning Source LLC
Chambersburg PA
CBHW071826020426
42331CB00007B/1627